Nuala and the ring of power

A story about a real girl

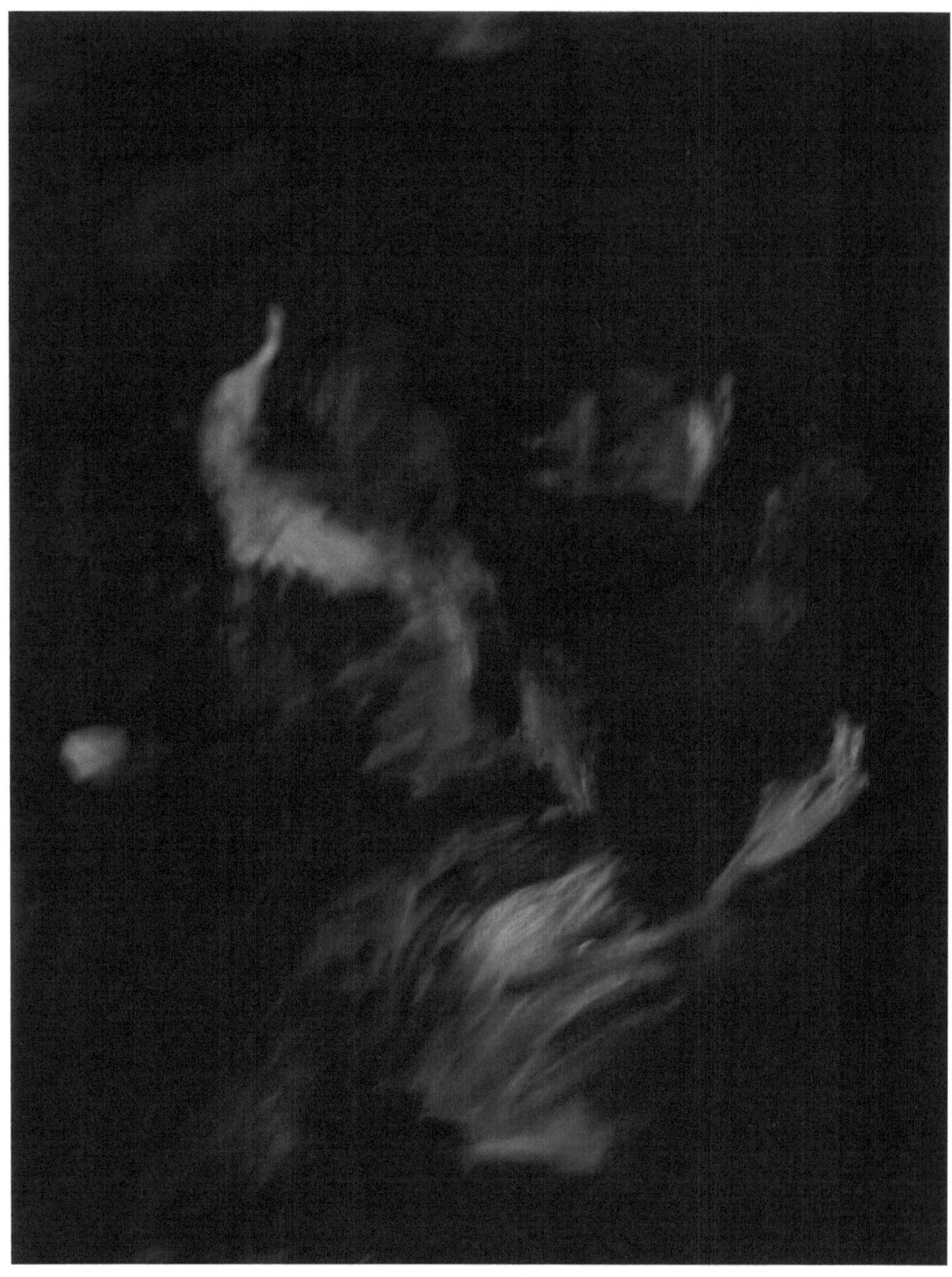

Nuala had run away from home.She ran and ran and she met a beggar who was bloodied and bandaged,
He gave her a ring and then ran.

Then she met a wolf.

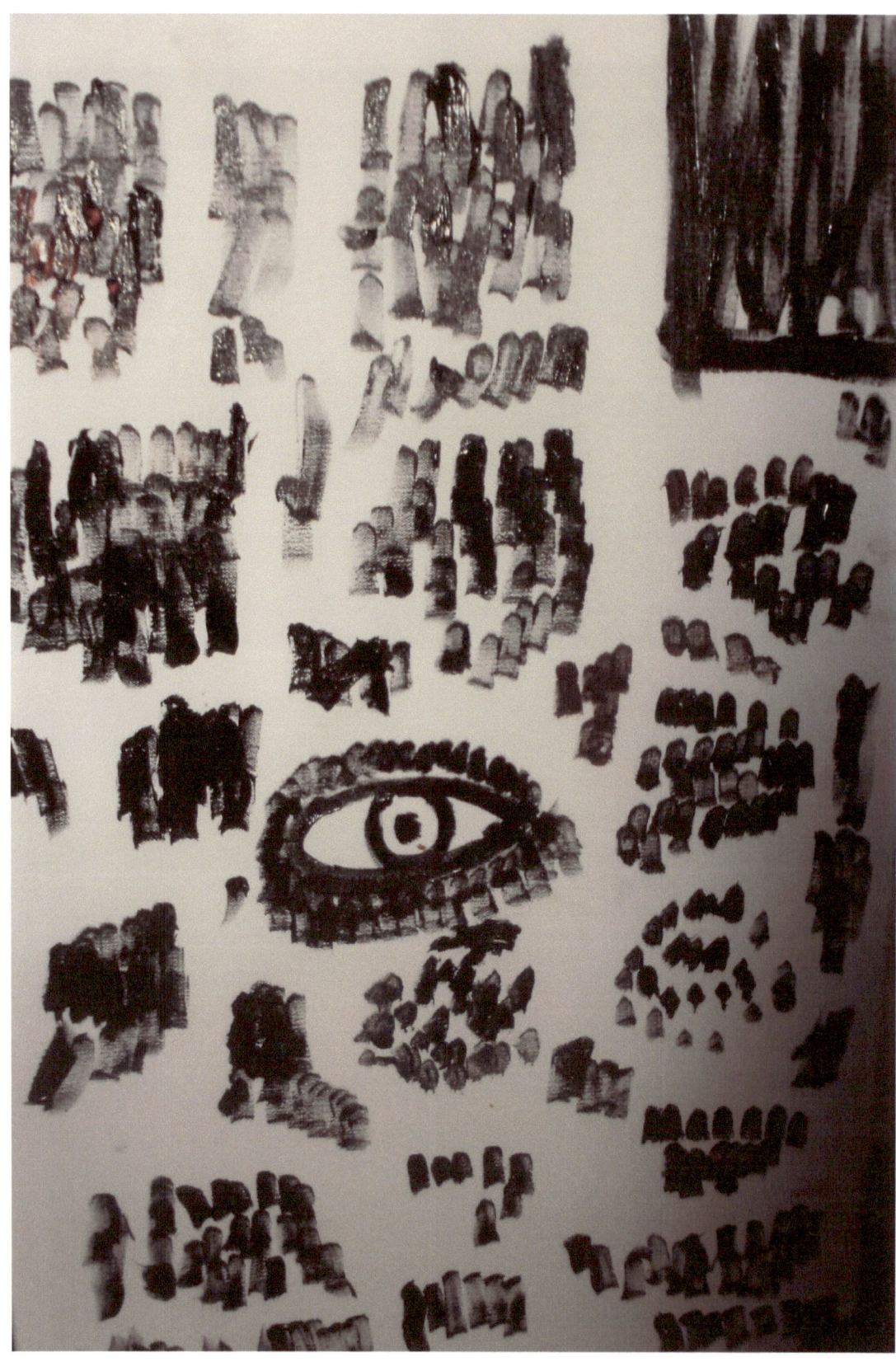

She had a vision of armies numbering a billion.

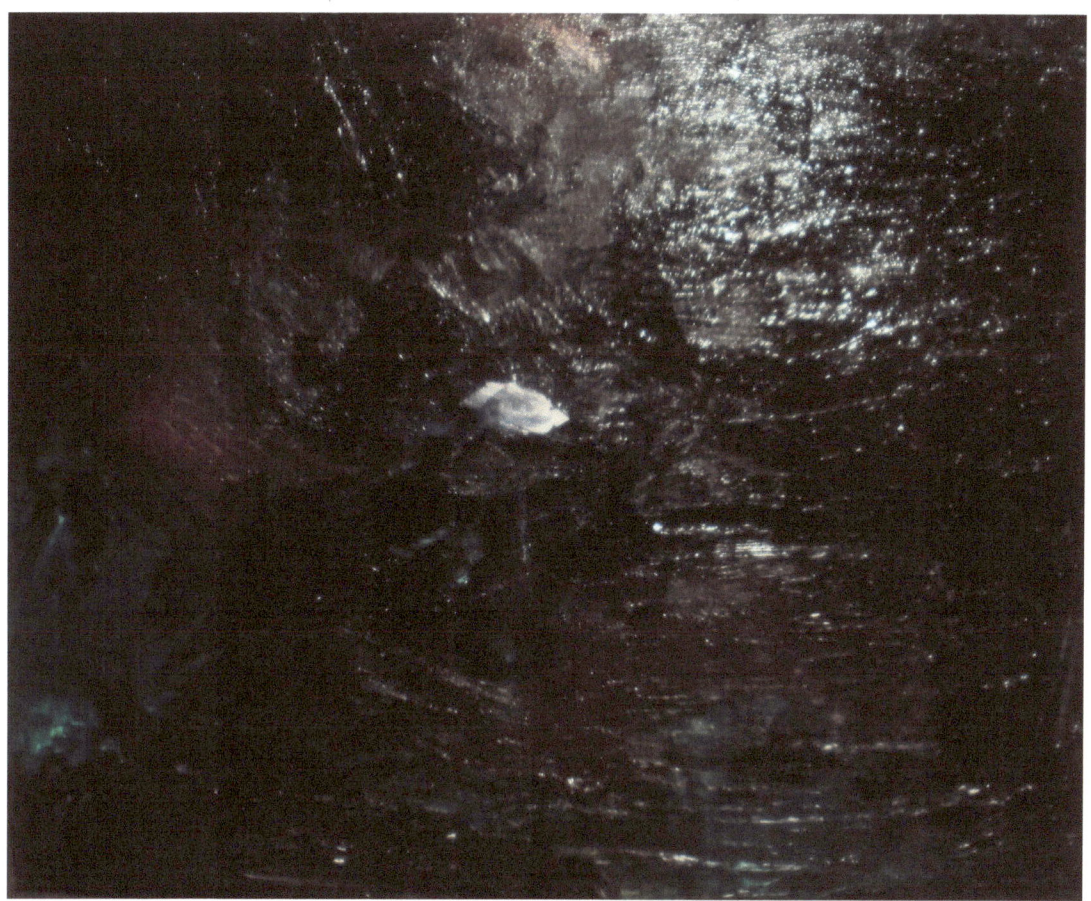

She heard the scream of white magic.

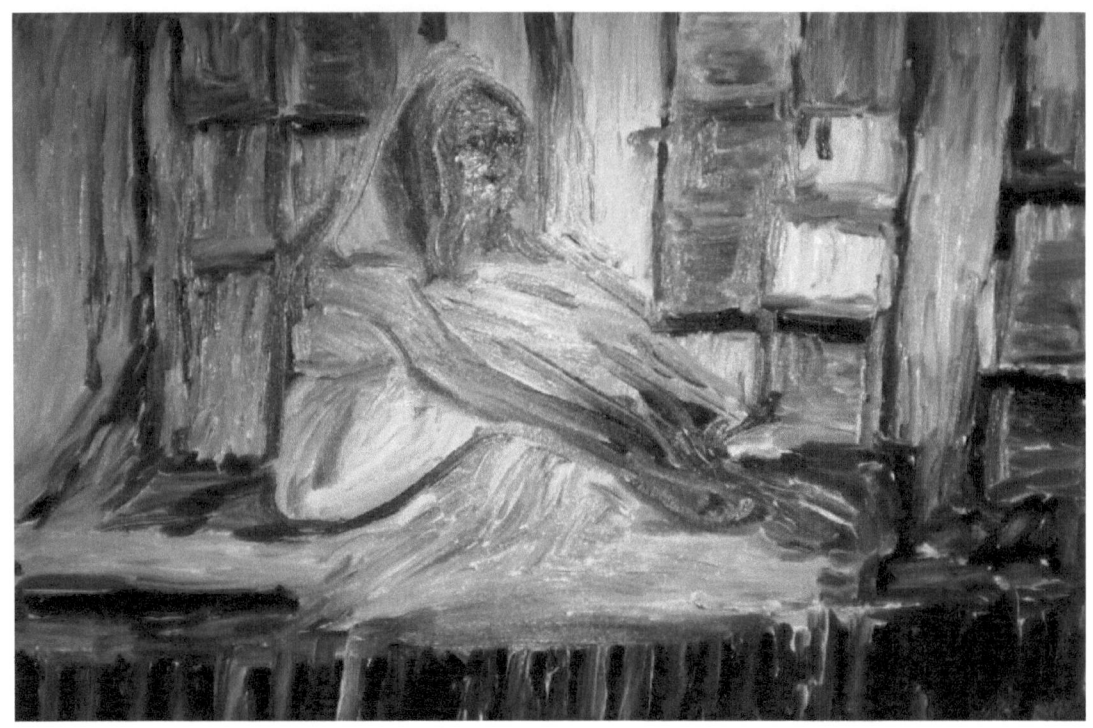

She went into an empty house and met a vampire.

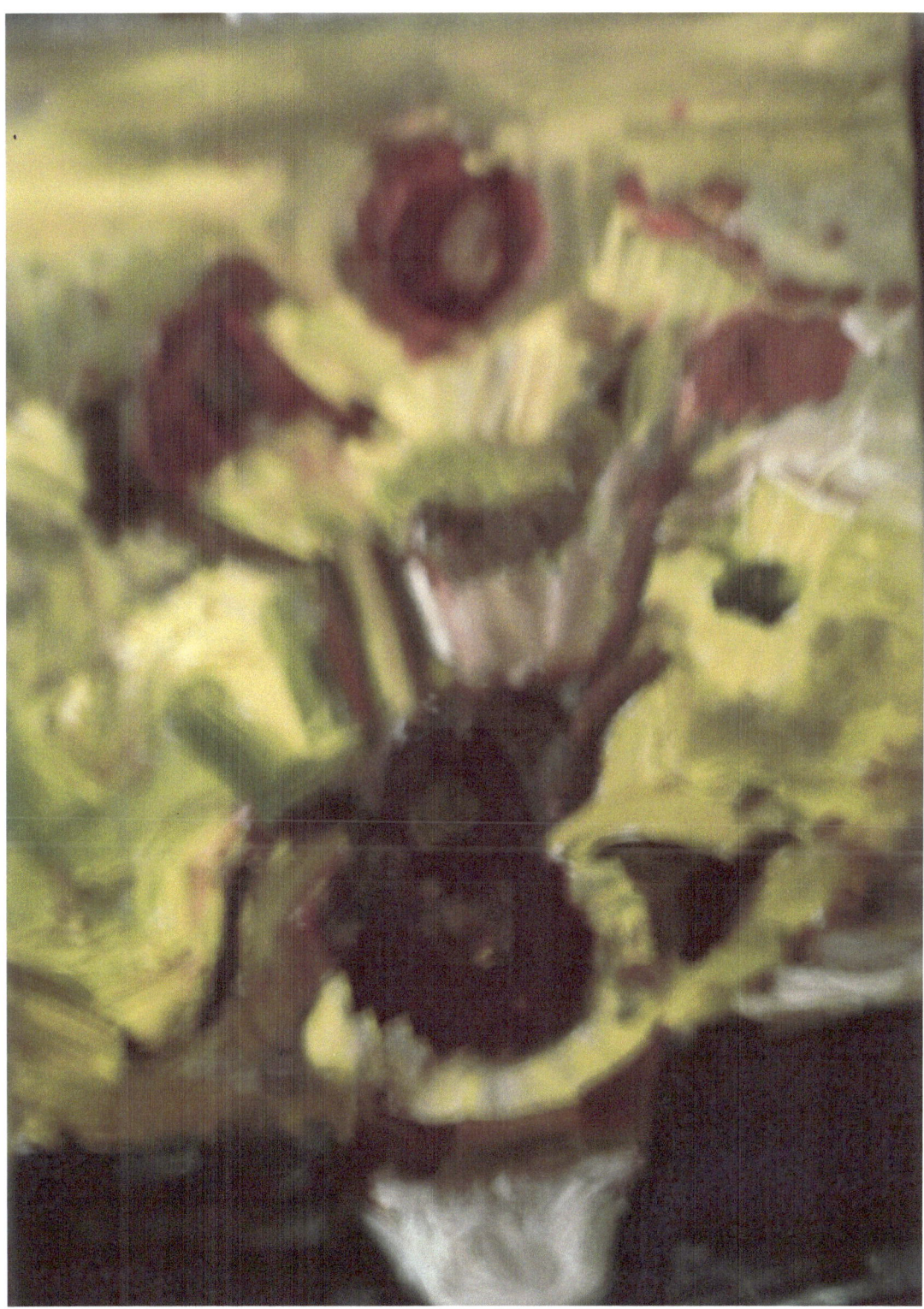

She ran and fell over a vase.

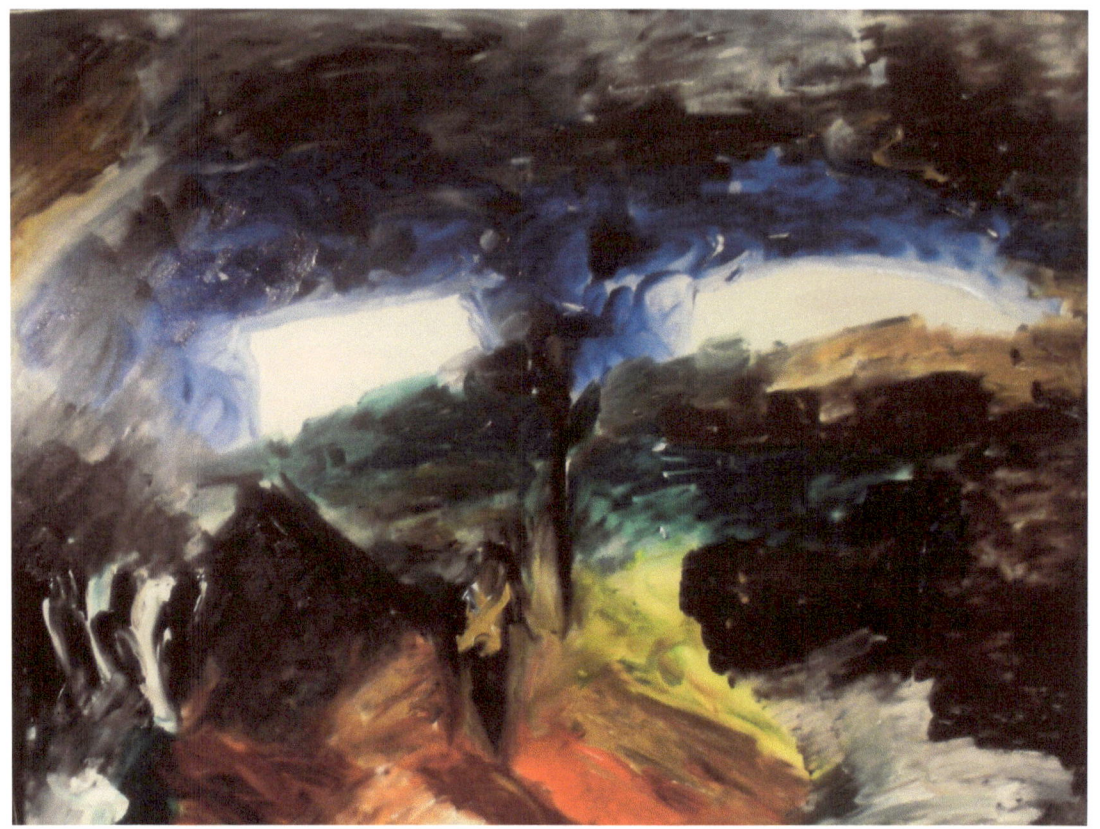

She met a soldier.True love he told her.

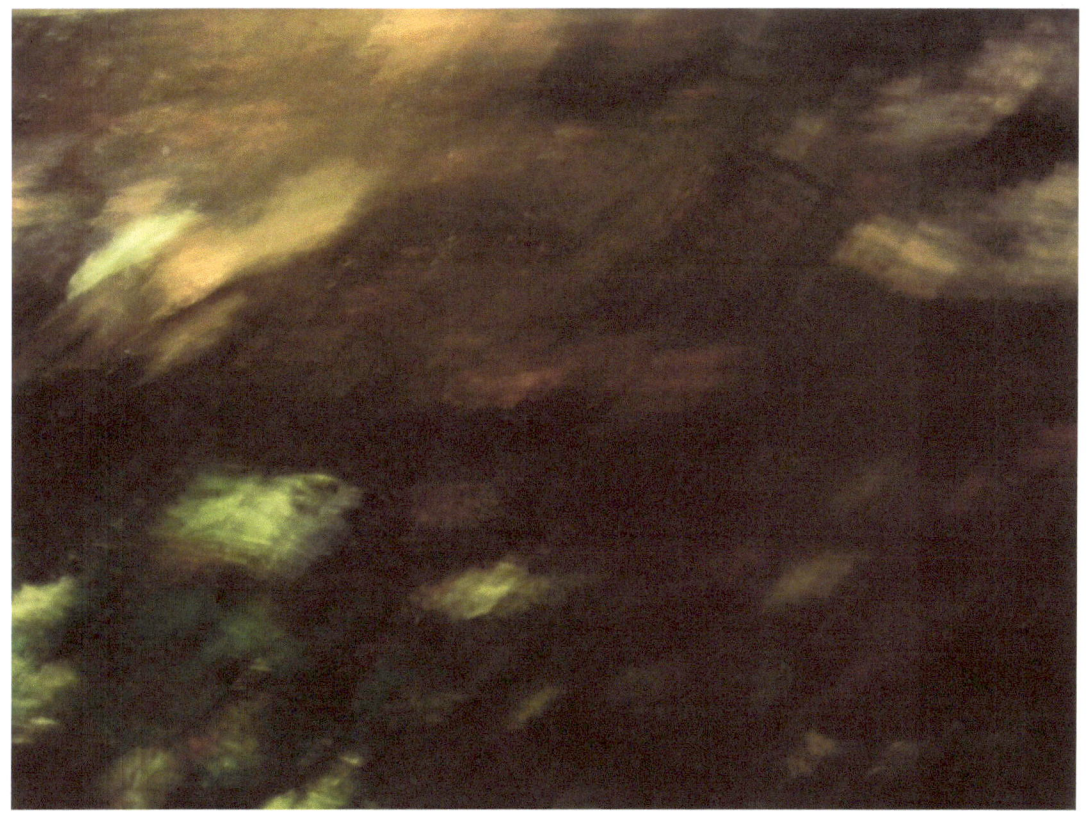

She saw volcano.

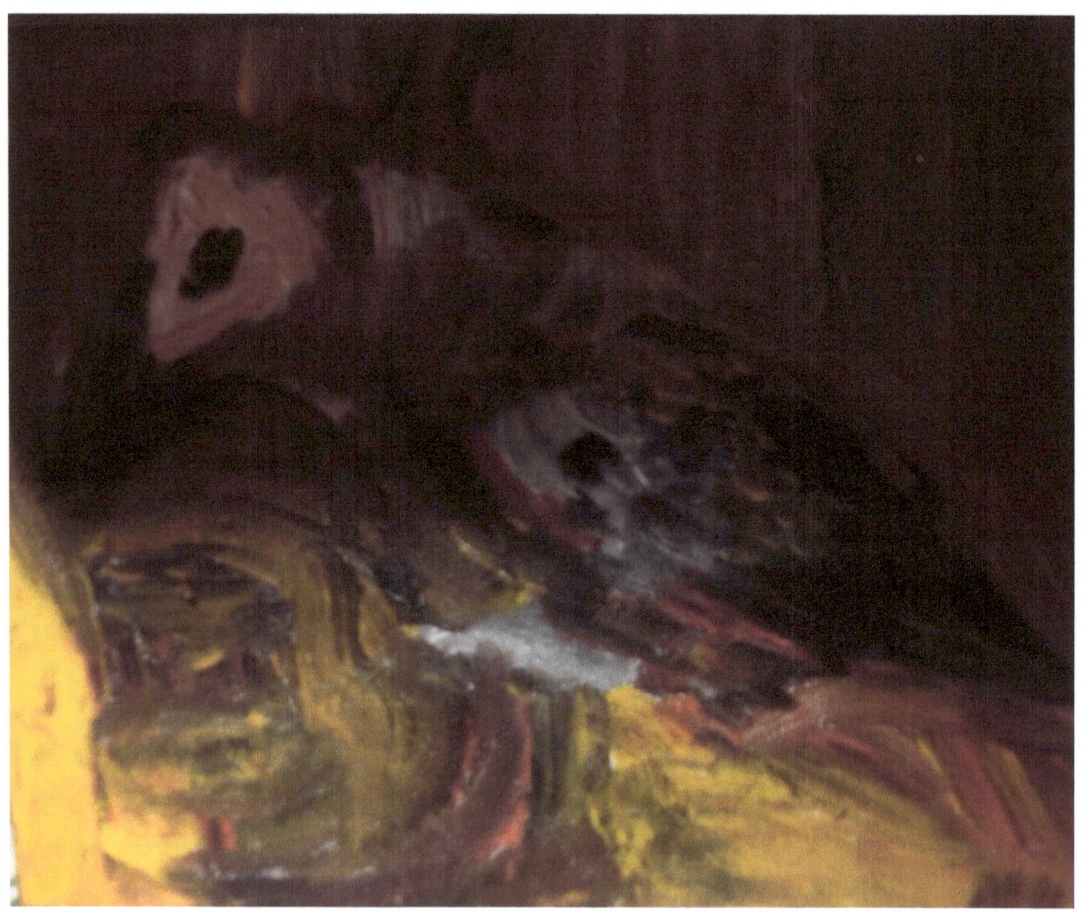
A seagull chick stood nearby

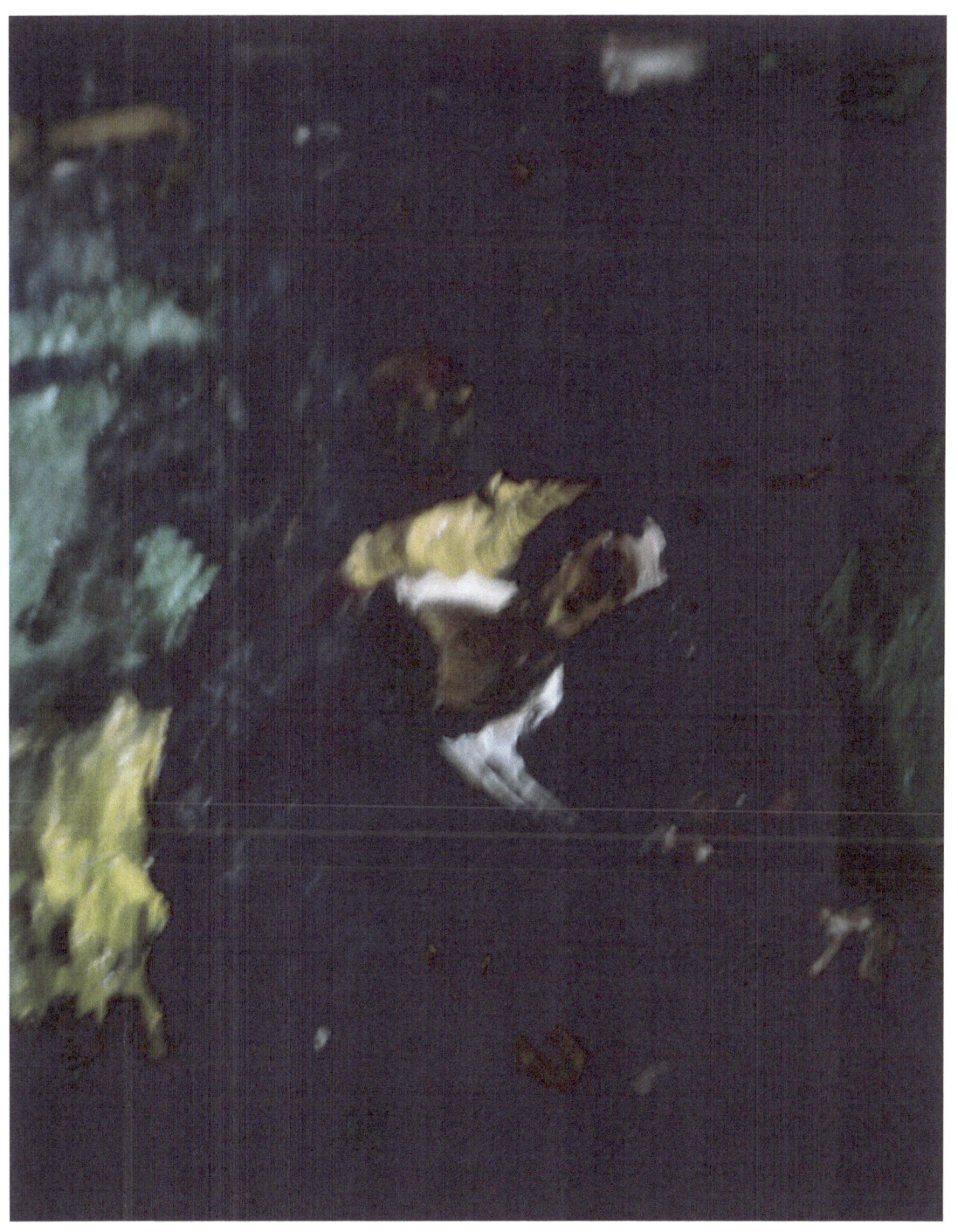

She saw a woman and a man take a child.She said nothing.

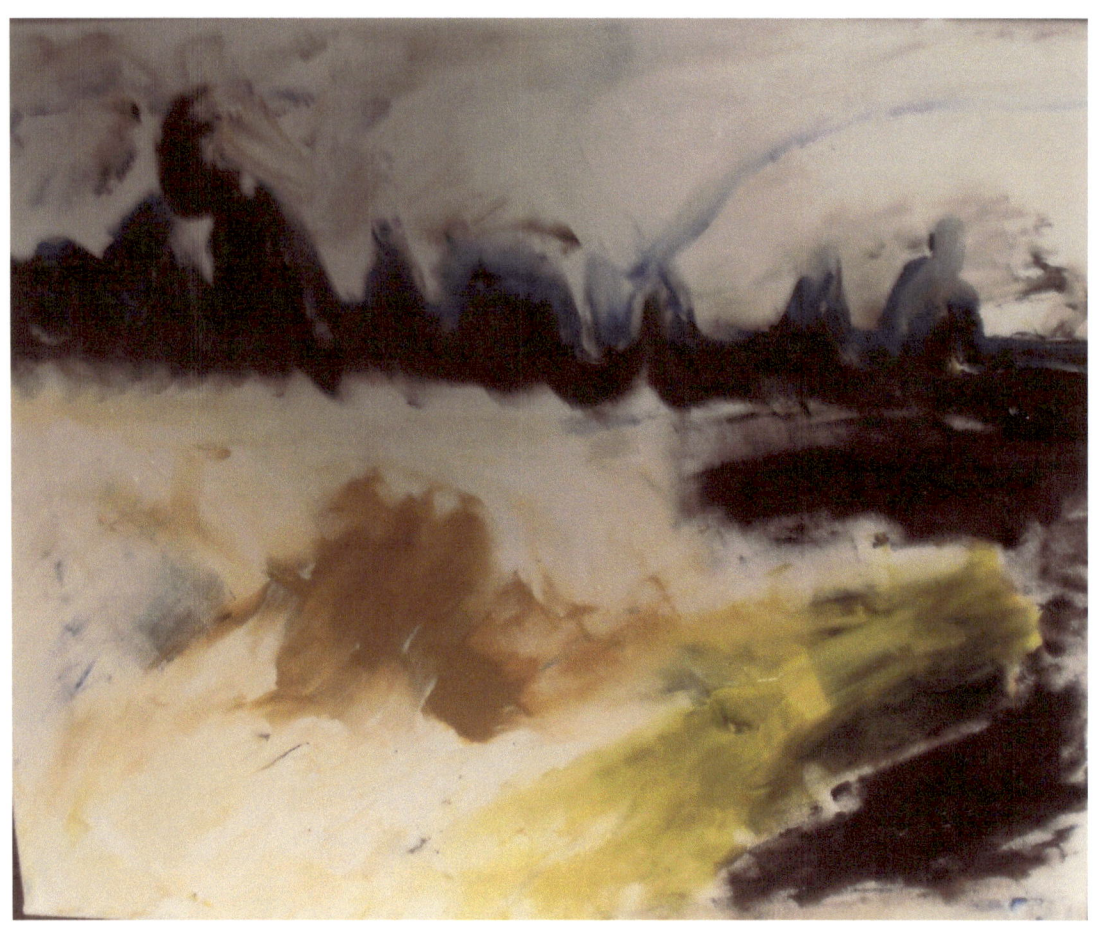

She ran past towns and villages.

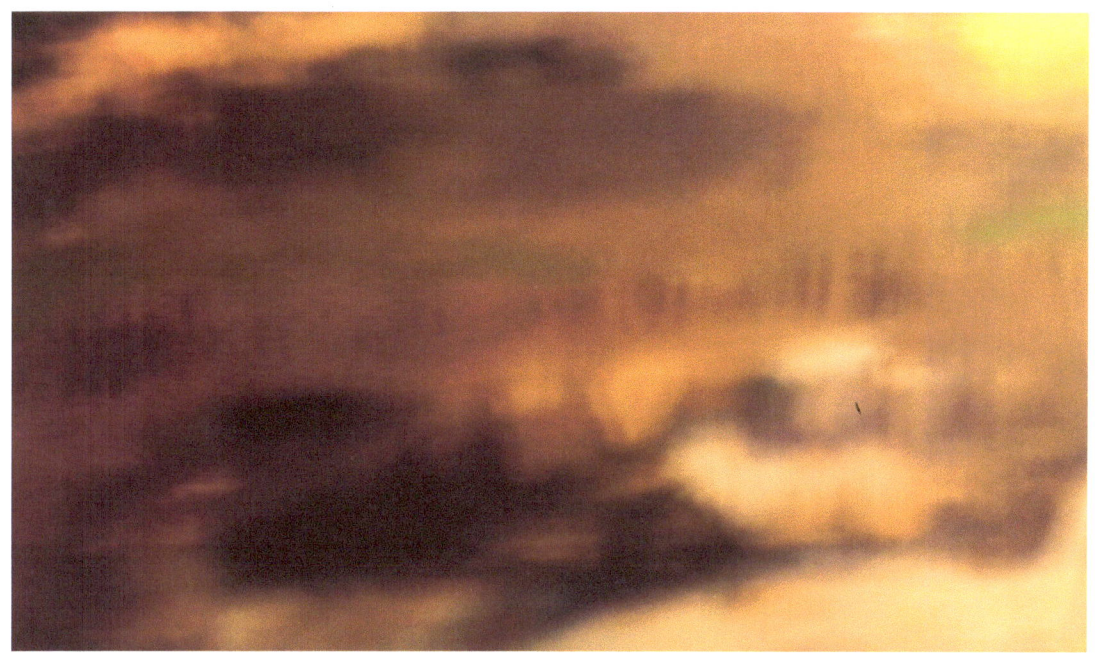

She went to London.It was on fire.

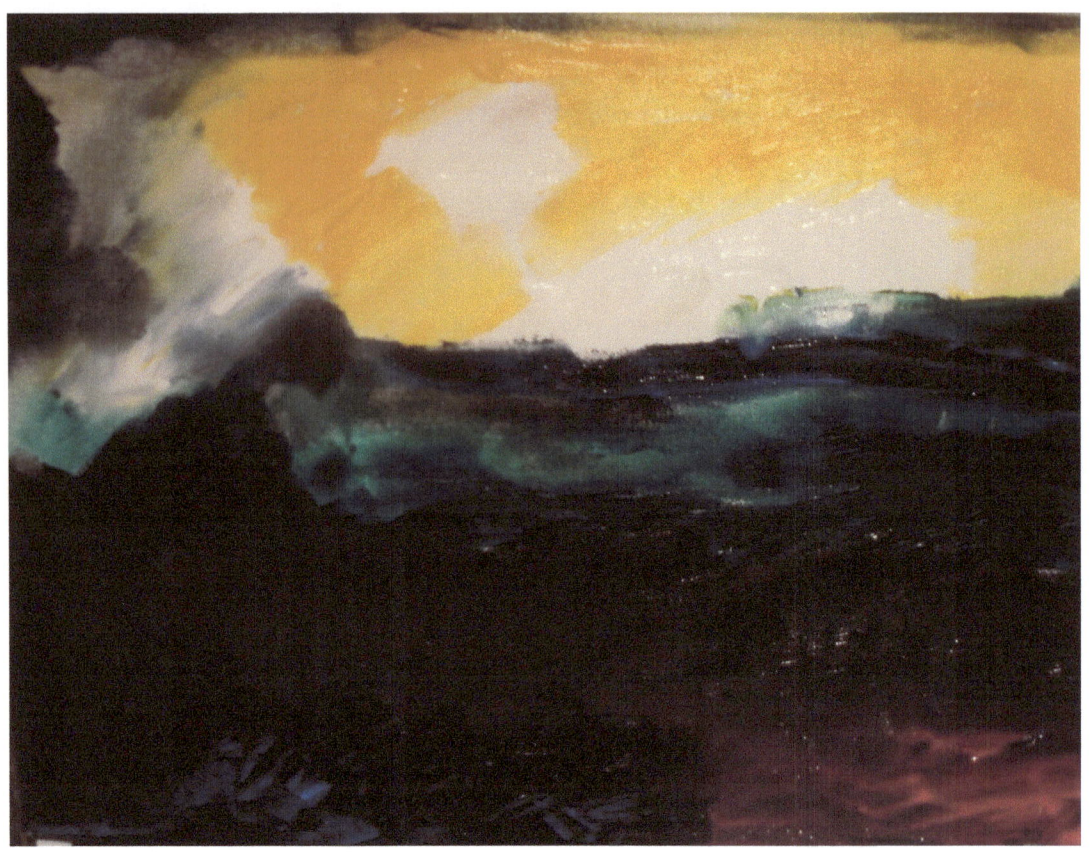

They told her there had been a nuclear bomb.

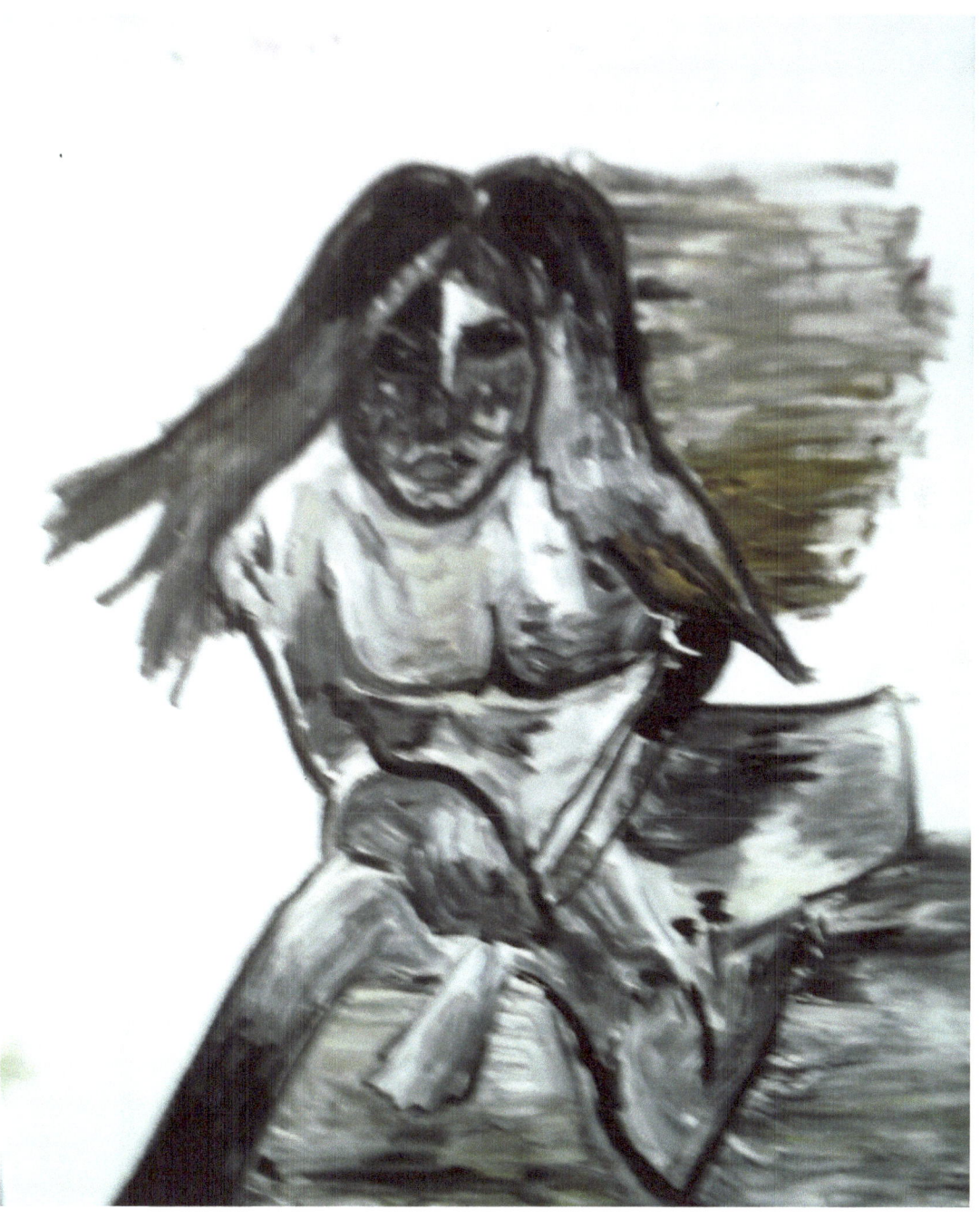

She did this.

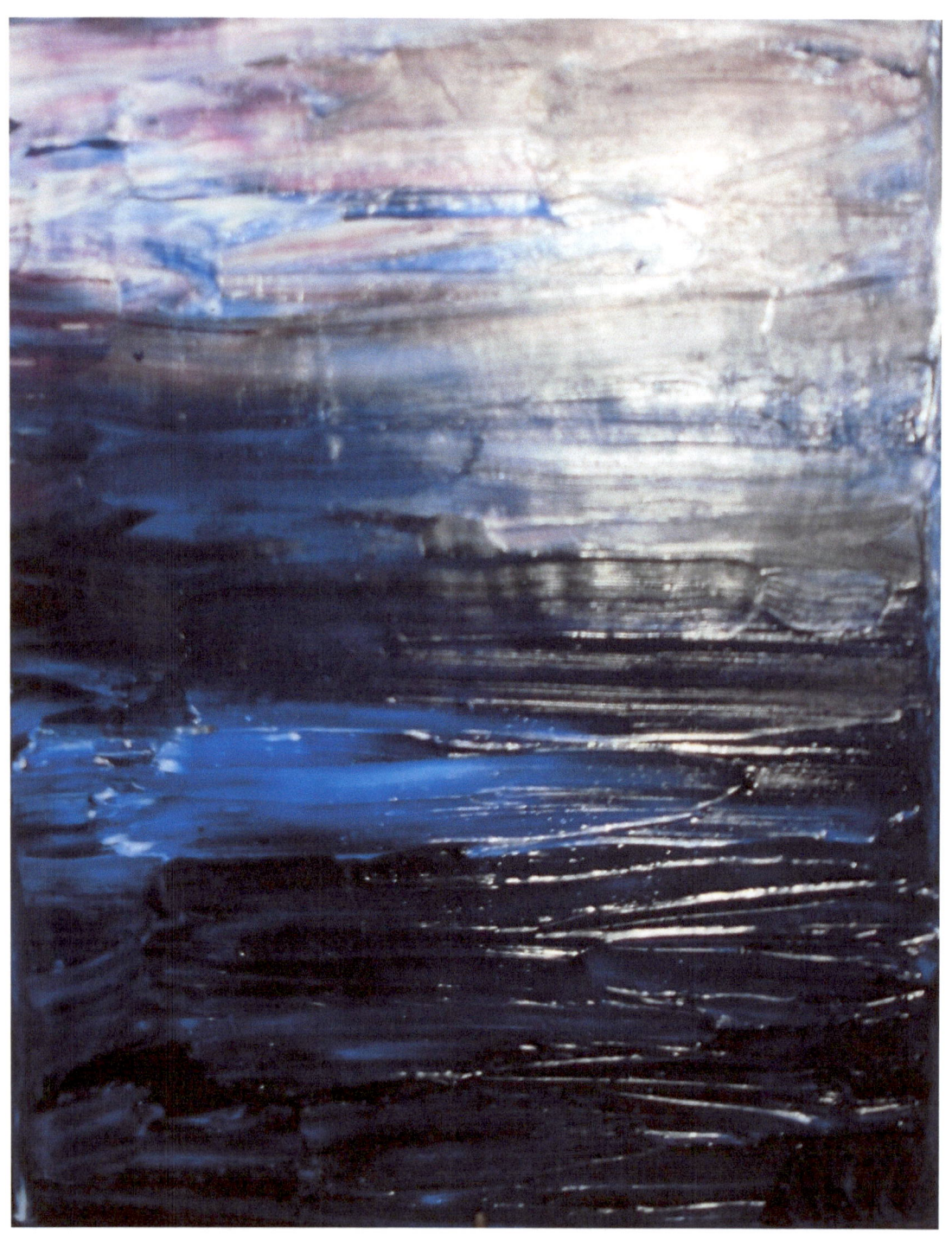

Someone said imagine there's no heaven.

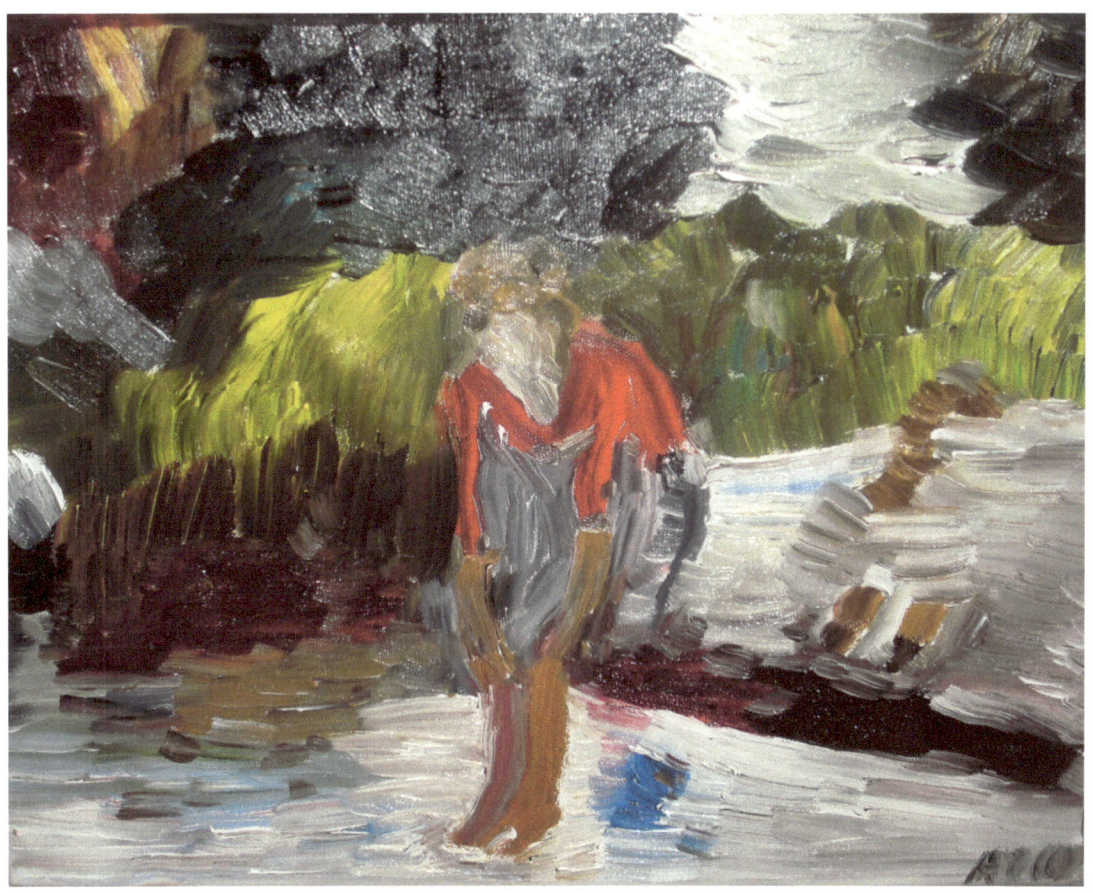

A woman said you've escaped then.

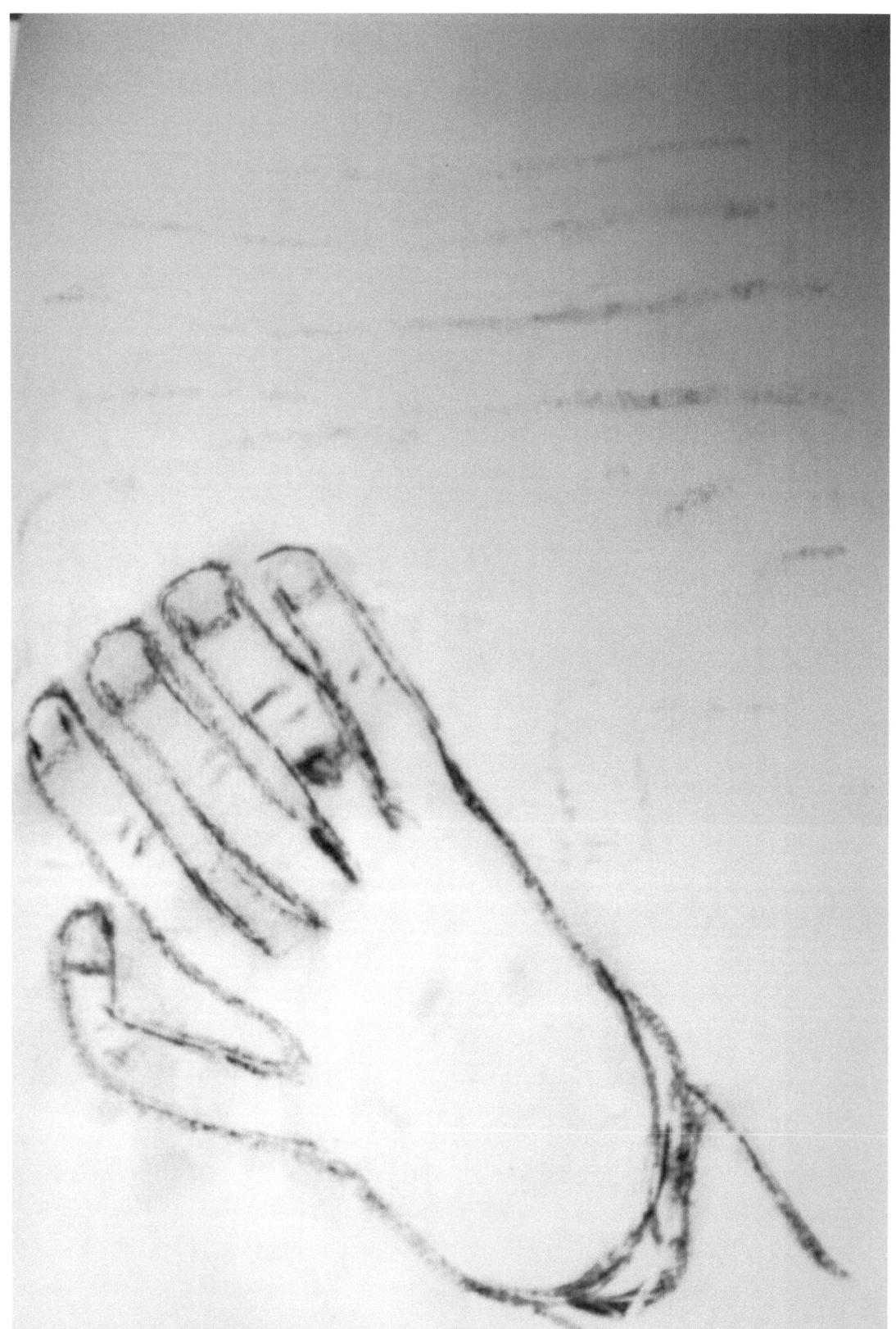

She said you have a nice ring.

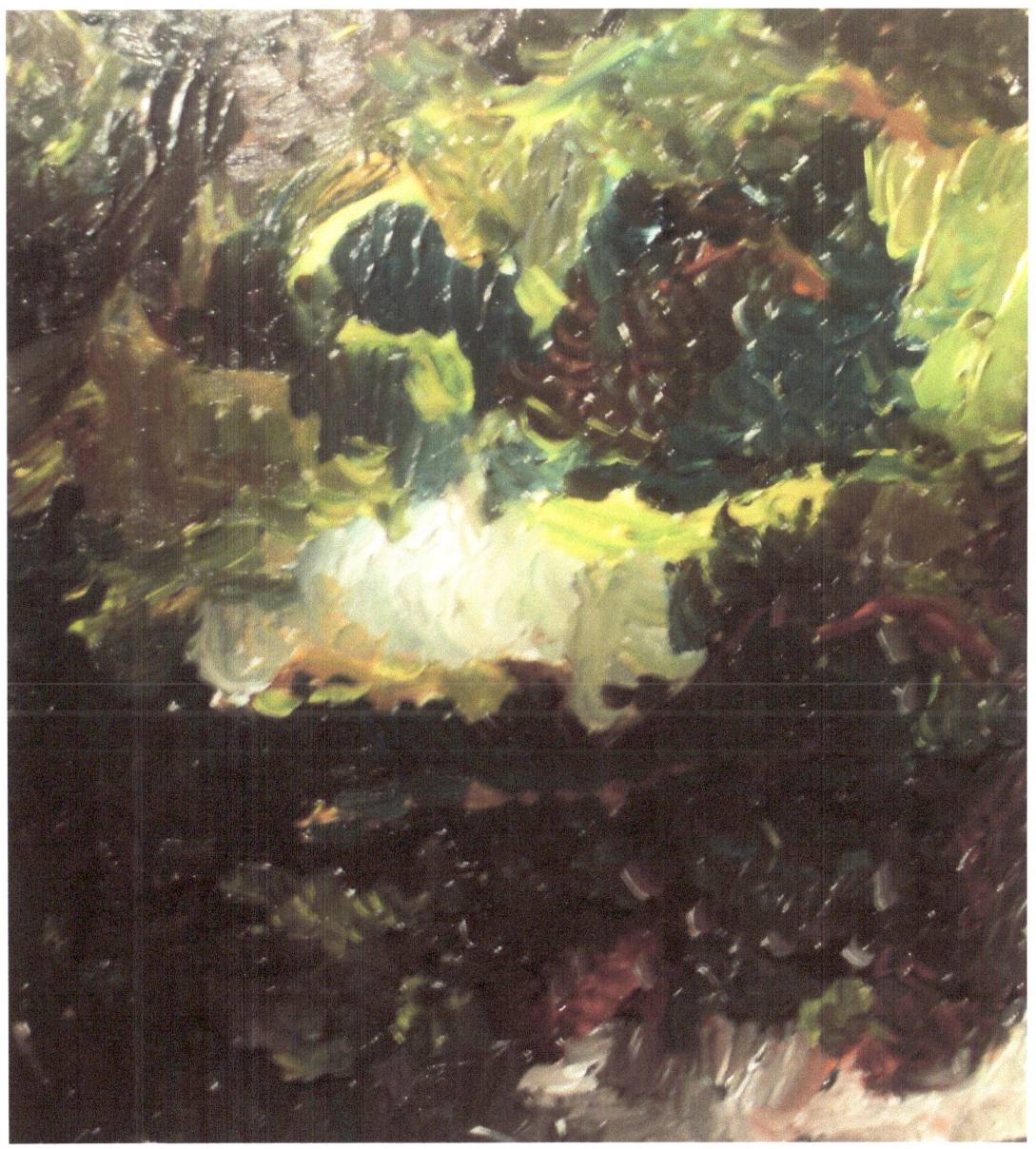

She used it the world turned to fire.

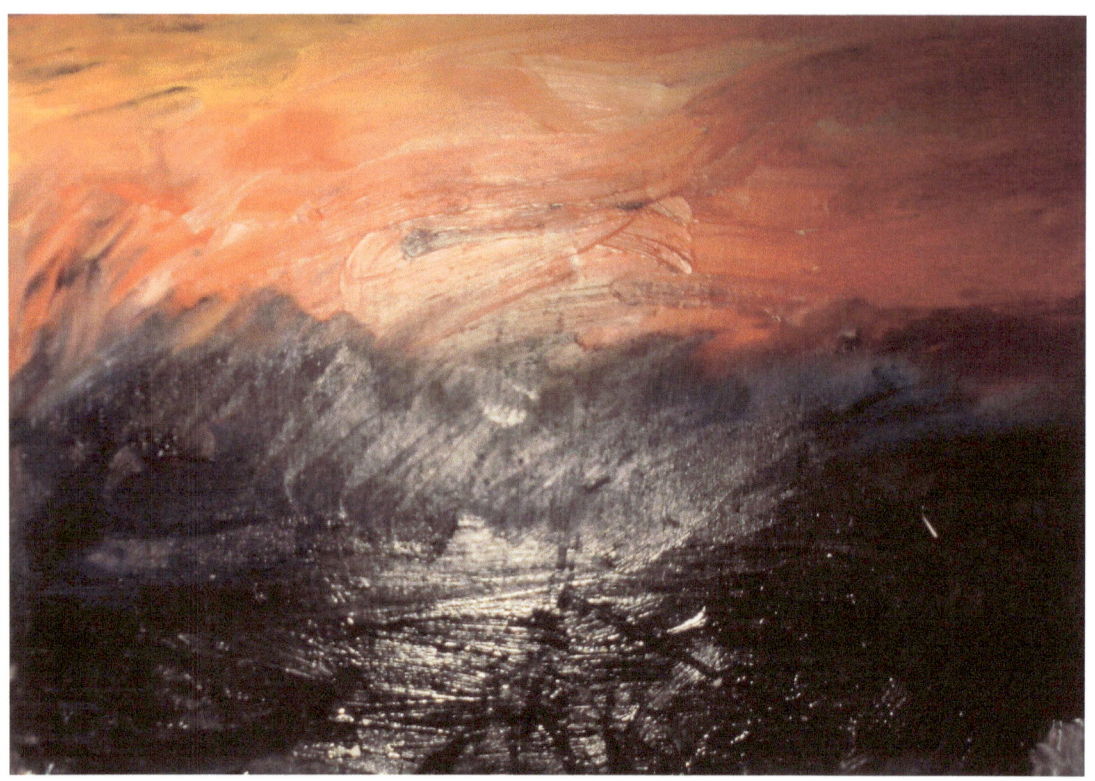

She took the ring off.Suddenly she was at home staring at a sunset.

www.ingramcontent.com/pod-product-compliance
Lightning Source LLC
Chambersburg PA
CBHW050437180526
45159CB00006B/2576